Punctuation
for Review
and Reference

A Style
Manual
with
Exercises

Edward Voeller

PASSPORT BOOKS
NTC/Contemporary Publishing Company

Library of Congress Cataloging-in-Publication Data

Voeller, Edward A.
      Punctuation for review and reference: a style manual with
exercises / Edward Voeller.
            p.   cm.
      Includes index.
      ISBN 0-8442-0817-5
      1. English language—Punctuation—Handbooks, manuals, etc.
2. English language—Punctuation—Problems, exercises, etc.
I. Title.
PE1450.V64   1997
428.2—dc21   97-38204
                                                              CIP

These materials were first developed by LanguagePower Publications.
Cover design by Amy Yu
Interior design by William Seabright and Associates

Published by Passport Books
An imprint of NTC/Contemporary Publishing Company
4255 West Touhy Avenue, Lincolnwood (Chicago), Illinois 60646-1975 U.S.A.
Printed in the United States of America
International Standard Book Number: 0-8442-0817-5
18   17   16   15   14   13   12   11   10   9   8   7   6   5   4   3   2   1

Contents

Introduction

Punctuation does not have many very vocal proponents; there are few people campaigning for the proper use of commas and colons. Other features of written communication fare much better; classroom time is always available for spelling, and every child has gone though several spelling books before finishing elementary school. The tiny marks of punctuation, on the other hand, are often taken for granted. Some usage manuals ignore the system of punctuation altogether, and others scatter rules throughout thick volumes.

Even professional writers sometimes give only casual attention to punctuation, yet no writer would omit punctuation marks altogether, and any reader would certainly balk at a paragraph devoid of commas, periods, and question marks. A paragraph with missing or misplaced punctuation includes the potential for miscommunication. Every writer and every reader knows that punctuation marks are essential.

Clear Expression, Efficient Reading

With the exception of correspondence, writing is usually one-way communication. It does not share many of the features of speech which serve to reinforce or confirm meaning, including facial expressions and gestures; stress and intonation; and the opportunity for immediate feedback from a listener. Writers must rely on other devices to make meaning clear, and among the most important is punctuation. Punctuation marks have serious responsibilities.

Unless a piece of writing is clear and easy to read, it may not be read willingly. Properly used, punctuation contributes to clarity and smooth and easy reading; incorrectly applied, punctuation may slow and distract the reader, drawing unnecessary attention to the punctuation marks and away from the meaning of the writing.

Good Punctuation

What is good punctuation? The foremost rule of punctuation is that it must promote clarity in writing, and that should be the first consideration in using punctuation marks. Clarity requires consistency, however, and that is the purpose of a reference manual that reflects a general consensus on the use of punctuation; the marks must have the same meaning to all readers.

Consistency is also important because there are occasions when there may be more than one way to punctuate a sentence for clarity. Editors recognize this, and they sometimes introduce small variations in punctuation style for their publications; also, British usage varies in a few minor ways from customary American style. Although a system of punctuation may have arbitrary features, there is no lack of agreement on the purpose of punctuation marks, and while two alternative styles may contribute equally to the clarity of writing, the consistent application of one style is important. One of the intentions of this book is to reflect a general agreement on the commonly accepted uses of the symbols of punctuation and to familiarize the student with that usage and to reinforce it.

Punctuation for Review and Reference

Punctuation for Review and Reference was designed for both new and experienced writers of English as a practice guide and reference manual. The book offers easy access to graded presentations of the punctuation system along with exercises for the development of essential skills in using and recognizing proper punctuation. *Punctuation for Review and Reference* is a three-part manual that moves from basic to more difficult features of punctuation, and though the student may begin at any point in the book, it may be helpful for the learner to practice the early lessons before going on to more challenging sections. The three parts of the book provide convenient goals by which students can perceive their progress.

Finally, *Punctuation for Review and Reference* provides a useful appendix with guides for punctuating bibliographies and letters, spelling rules, a list of words that are sometimes confused by both new and experienced writers, and answers to the punctuation exercises.

A Note for Teachers

Some of the exercises in *Punctuation for Review and Reference* may be done in the book; others require the student to write sentences on a separate piece of paper. However, some teachers may want their students to keep a notebook in which they complete all of the exercises from the book. This provides a convenient way to grade a student's work, and it keeps the book clean in the event it must be used by others.

Part One

CAPITALIZATION 1; PERIOD 1

Capitalize the first word of a sentence. Use a period at the end of a sentence.

Capital letters and periods are very important.

Requests and commands also usually require a period.

Don't forget to call me.
Please be on time.

A period is not necessary with titles of publications, films, or songs, even if they are sentences.

My Name Is Aram by William Saroyan
This Is My Story by Eleanor Roosevelt
The Heart Is a Lonely Hunter by Carson McCullers

---

1 Write each group of words as a sentence. Capitalize the first word and use a period at the end of each sentence.
- my new English class begins at eight o'clock
- it lasts one hour
- there are students from seven countries in the class
- our teacher has two rules
- don't be late for class
- please leave the classroom quietly

2 Unscramble each string of words below to make a sentence.
   Capitalize the first word and use a period at the end of each sentence.

- homework us gives our teacher every day
- homework I do in my the library
- reading we *My Name Is Aram* are
- don't TV for I time have
- this lesson trouble with am having I
- this me with help please

CAPITALIZATION 2

Capitalize certain words, including personal names, the pronoun *I*, and kinship words as names;

> José Martinez, Mother, Aunt Edna, Papa
> *But:* my mother, my sister Stella, your dad

titles with personal names;

> Prime Minister Li; Professor Martin Feller, Ph.D.; Mr. Yamada
> *But:* the dentist; Martin Feller, professor of journalism; Robert Broussard, mayor of Montréal; Harri Holkeri, prime minister of Finland; the capitalization of titles is optional with very prominent persons: Harri Holkeri, Prime Minister of Finland

names of continents, countries, cities, and similar kinds of places;

> Asia; South America; the Republic of France; Mombasa, Kenya; the Gopher State; New York City
> *But:* the city of New York, the western states, the UN countries

names of buildings, structures, and streets;

> the Golden Gate Bridge, the CN Tower, Lincoln High School, the Pyramids, Fifth Avenue, the Tower Medical Building
> *But:* the library, my high school, the streets of Paris

names of institutions, businesses, organizations, and official government offices;

the United Nations; Harvard University; IBM, Inc.;
the International Red Cross; the Giants Baseball Club;
the United States Senate; the Supreme Court;
the Department of Education
But: a baseball team, a university, the court

nationalities, cultures, languages, and religions and religious names;

Hawaiian, Asian, French, Islam, Hindi, Buddhist, the Koran, God
But: french fries, dutch treat, blacks and whites

days of the week, months, holidays;

Monday, February, New Year's Day
But: eastern standard time, spring, summer, fall, autumn, winter

names of mountains, rivers, islands, and oceans and the names of other places on the globe;

the Atlantic Ocean, the Mississippi River, Mount Everest,
Lake Superior, the Hawaiian Islands
But: island, river, lake, sea

names of commonly recognized areas and specific places;

the Near East, North Africa, Southeast Asia, the South Pole,
the Western Hemisphere, the South (in the United States), Earth
But: the earth, the sun, the south of England, northern India,
north, south, east, west

special events and historical events and eras.

the World Cup, World War II, the Battle of Waterloo,
the Meiji Restoration, the Ming Dynasty
But: the two world wars, the twentieth century

Categories or kinds or types of things are usually not capitalized.

a vocational school, aspirin, a station wagon, a terrier
But: Lassie, a Toyota

Titles of publications are also capitalized. (See Capitalization 3.)

PUNCTUATION FOR REVIEW AND REFERENCE

3 Some of the words in the following sentences should be capitalized. Circle the first letter of those words.

- it's easy to find our high school.
- go down this street, and turn left at the city hall.
- then drive across the river on riverside bridge.
- the school is on the northwest corner of winter street and freeway 94.
- you'll see the new northfield municipal stadium opposite the school.
- you can park under the large oak tree on the north side of the school.

APOSTROPHE 1

An apostrophe (') is used to replace letters omitted in contractions. The words *be*, *have*, some modals, and the negative *not* are sometimes contracted with personal pronouns, the pronoun *that*, some question words, and the words *here* and *there*. Some common contractions are given below.

be
I am → I'm; you are → you're;   he is → he's; she is → she's
it is → it's; we are → we're;   they are → they're
who is → who's; what is → what's; where is → where's;
how is → how's; that is → that's; there is → there's;
here is → here's

have
I have → I've; you have → you've; he has → he's;
she has → she's
it has → it's; we have → we've; they have → they've
who has → who's; who have → who've
where has → where's; where have → where've
that has → that's; there has → there's; there have → there've

had
I had → I'd; you had → you'd; he had → he'd; she had → she'd
it had → it'd; we had → we'd; they had → they'd
there had → there'd; where had → where'd; who had → who'd

4

modals
Will and *would* may be contracted with pronouns and with
    the question words *where* and *who*:
I will → I'll; where will → where'll; that will → that'll
I would → I'd; where would → where'd; that would → that'd
Have is sometimes contracted with *could, should,*
    and other modals:
could have → could've; also, *should've, must've, would've*

negatives with *be, do,* and *have*
is not → isn't; are not → aren't; *But: am not* is never contracted
was not → wasn't; were not → weren't
does not → doesn't; do not → don't; did not → didn't
has not → hasn't; have not → haven't; had not → hadn't

negatives with modals
will not → won't; would not → wouldn't
can not → can't; could not → couldn't
must not → mustn't; should not → shouldn't

Certain pairs of words look the same when they are contracted.
Would and *had*, for example, are both contracted as *'d*, and *has* and *is*
are contracted as *'s*. *I'd* can be a contraction of *I had* or *I would*, and
he's can mean *he is* or *he has*. **Examples:** *If I'd known he was
unemployed, I'd have tried to help him find a job. He's lived here a
year, and he's still looking for a job.*

Some writers make the mistake of using *I better* instead of *I'd better* or *I
had better*, and *could of* instead of *could've* or *could have*. The following
words are also sometimes confused: *it's* and *its*; *you're* and *your*; *they're,
their*, and *there*; *there's* and *theirs*; *who's* and *whose*; and *lets* and *let's*.
Lets is a form of the verb *let*, which means "allow," and *let's* is the contraction of *let us*. Also, the word *yours* is sometimes incorrectly written
as *your's*; there is no contracted form *your's*.

Contractions may be used in informal letters to friends, and contractions
are also used to write what someone has said. However, contractions are
not used very much in formal writing, and they should generally not be
used in papers for school or for business.

4 Write the two uncontracted words for each of the contracted forms that are underlined in the following sentences.

· Ali <u>hasn't</u> written to his parents in a long time.
· <u>He's</u> been very busy.
· He <u>can't</u> call home because <u>it's</u> too expensive.
· <u>You'd</u> better let him call from your office.
· <u>He'd</u> like that.
· <u>I'll</u> tell him as soon as <u>I've</u> finished my work here.

COMMA 1

Use a comma before *and*, *but*, *or*, and *nor* when those words are used to connect two sentences or independent clauses. A comma may also be used before *so* and *yet* when they are used like conjunctions to connect two sentences.

> The express to Helsinki is fast, and it is not very expensive.
> The plane is faster, but the train is more relaxing.
> We can take a taxi to the airport, or we can take a bus.
> There aren't any nonstop flights, nor are there any
>   flights on Sundays.
> The flight leaves at 9:50, so let's hurry.
> The airport bus is usually crowded, yet I think we can get seats.

A comma is not used with a conjunction if the two independent clauses are very short.

> Marc flew and I took the train.

A comma is often not used if the subject in the initial clause is not repeated in the second portion of the sentence.

> Flight 55 departs at nine on weekdays and at 10:10
>   on weekends.
> We'll leave here at six-thirty and get to the airport at
>   around 7:25.

Always use a comma to introduce contrasting information.

> The flight stops in Bonn on weekdays, but not on weekends.

Sentences may not be joined with only a comma. Use a conjunction and a comma.

> *Incorrect:* The flight was crowded, the service was good.
> *Correct:* The flight was crowded, but the service was good.
> *Correct:* The flight was crowded. The service was good.

A conjunction should generally not be the first word of a sentence.

> *Incorrect:* Economy class is crowded. And the food is terrible.
> *Incorrect:* First class is comfortable. But it is rather expensive.
> *Correct:* Economy class is crowded, and the food is terrible.
> *Correct:* First class is comfortable, but it is rather expensive.

---

5 In which of the following are commas and periods used correctly? Draw a line through the incorrect examples.

- I like this city, I like this neighborhood.
- The winters are mild. The summers are cool.
- The shopping mall is not far from here, and it is easy to park there.
- The subway system here is very convenient, the fare is not very expensive.
- My children can walk to school, or they can take the bus.
- The public pool is not far. Nor is it ever crowded.

6 Combine the following into sentences using *and*, *but*, *or*, *so*, and *yet*. Use commas where necessary.

- The city services are good + the taxes are high here.
- The municipal zoo is free + it is near our home.
- There is little crime in this city + we are not afraid to go out alone at night.
- People here drive slowly + carefully.
- City employees can work from seven to three + they can work from nine to five.
- City employees have many days of vacation + their salaries are very good.

APOSTROPHE 2

Use an apostrophe (') or an apostrophe -*s* (-'*s*) to form the possessive.
Add -'*s* to singular words and to most names.

> the little girl's purse   a friend's advice   Hiroshi's new car

The possessive -'*s* is also added to singular words that end with
an -*s* sound.

> the actress's first movie   Paris's traffic   Los Angeles's population
> Professor Jones's lectures   my boss's car
> *Exception:* no -s is added to the possessive form *Kansas'*.

Add an apostrophe to most plural nouns and to plural forms of names.

> the students' schedules   the Browns' house
> our parents' money

Use -'*s* with plural nouns that do not end in -*s*.

> the children's toys   women's fashions

Two related nouns are usually punctuated like one noun.

> Mom and Dad's anniversary
> Note the double possessive: a friend of John's
> a cousin of mine

The possessive -'*s* cannot always be expressed naturally with *of*;
for example, *the purse of the little girl* is not very likely to be heard
in English. On the other hand, some possessive expressions are natural
with *of* and unnatural with -'*s*; *the top of the shelf* is more natural than
the shelf's top, for example. It is natural in English to say *the teacher
of the class*; however, *the car of John* is not natural.

In addition to the possessive -'*s* and *of* to indicate that two nouns are
related, a noun may sometimes modify another noun as an adjective.
Common examples are *a teachers college, a university campus, a school
festival, a computer program, a college library*. Nouns as adjectives
often answer the question *what kind?* or *which?*

7 **Study the examples, and then change the unnatural phrases below so that a noun is used as an adjective. EXAMPLES: Not** *tennis's shoes*, **but** *tennis shoes*. **Not a** *computer's desk*, **but a** *computer desk*.
· Not a kitchen's table, but _____ · Not a bicycle's wheel, but _____ · Not a fruit's basket, but _____ · Not a newspaper's subscription, but _____ · Not a basketball's coach, but _____ · Not a video's tape, but _____

8 **Add an apostrophe (') or an apostrophe -s (-'s) where necessary in the following groups of words.**
· Mr. Kim new book · the dogs owner · the Smiths property · a motorcycle helmet · the bottom shelves · a library card · my books · a road map · France history · the buses (or busses) drivers · a sports magazine · Bess things

COMMA 2

Use a comma after an item when it is one in a series of three or more items in a sentence. Notice that a comma is used before the words *and* and *or* in the following examples.

> The doctor told me not to swim, ride a bicycle, or drive a car.
> My car, my bicycle, and my scuba gear are for sale.
> He told me to listen to music, read books, or get a hobby.
> The doctor recommended vitamin C, iron, and zinc.
> *But:* I have to lose weight and get more sleep.

9 **Use commas in the sentences that require them.**
· I'm jogging now on Mondays Wednesdays and Fridays.
· Playing tennis skiing and bowling are three healthful activities.
· I don't smoke or drink coffee anymore.
· I get a lot of exercise and I go to bed early.
· I eat a lot of vegetables but I don't like celery broccoli or onions.

QUESTION MARK 1

Use a question mark with questions.

> What's your name?   Are you from Hong Kong?   You are?

---

10 **Write out the following dialogue using question marks and periods where necessary. Use capital letters where they are required.**
- that new student is from Sri Lanka
- he is
- yes, he is
- can he speak English
- what do you think
- when are you going to introduce me to him

COMMA 3

Use a comma with introductory words and phrases, such as *actually, anyway, as you know, basically, frankly, frankly speaking, in fact,* and *to tell the truth.* (See also transitional expressions in Comma 6 and 8.)

> I can't understand my teacher. Actually, nobody can understand him.
> I like my math teacher. In fact, I took the class because of her.

---

11 **Rewrite the sentences below using commas with conjunctions and introductory expressions. Use periods and capital letters where necessary. Some of the items may be more than one sentence.**
- Basically there is no problem with your work but you are late for class too often.
- I wonder if you could take notes for me in class on Monday as you know I can't come to school next week.
- Tuesday's test was difficult in fact I think I failed it.
- I can't afford to buy the textbook for class anyway the teacher said it is not required.

- I'd like to skip chemistry lab today actually I'd like to skip math class too.
- Mr. Brown is unpopular with the students yet he is an internationally famous teacher.

COMMA 4

Use commas with dates.

February 3, 1983   December 16, 1978
August 28, 1976   Friday, May 1st

No comma is used after the name of a month when it is followed immediately by the year, nor is a comma used in a date written in the international style.

April 1994   8 February 1946

A comma is normally used after a date in a sentence. However, if the expression with a comma is brief, the comma may be omitted. (See also Comma 5.)

The event of February 8, 1946, was a high point in her life.

Commas are also used between units of three digits with figures of one thousand and greater.

1,000   12,000   500,000   1,000,000

---

12 Use commas where they are required in the following sentences.
- My birthday is on January 23 and my wife's birthday is on January 22.
- Anna-Marie was born on the 16th of December but we had a party for her on the 20th.
- My best friend was born on a Saturday in February in 1956.
- Three people in my English class were born on the 23rd of this month but one was born in 1976 and the other two were born in 1975.

- I'm having a birthday party on the 19th and I'm sending you an invitation.
- I thought he was born on January 16 1920 but he was born on January 16 1919.

PERIOD 2

Use a period with most abbreviations, including personal titles;

Mr., Mrs., and Dr.
But: Ms and Miss do not require periods.

initials of a person's name;

E. Hemingway, T. S. Eliot

days of the week and months, except May, June, and July;

Sun. Mon. Tues. Wed. Thurs. Fri. Sat.
Jan. Feb. Mar. Apr. Aug. Sept. Oct. Nov. Dec.

time of day;

A.M., P.M., or a.m., p.m.; hr., min., sec.
But: M (noon), or m

countries and states;

U.K., Minn., N.Y., Ia.,
But: Periods are not used with the post office abbreviations of American states: MN, NY, IA

business designations;

Co. (company), Inc. (incorporated), Ltd. (limited)

units of measure. However, no periods are used with abbreviations of metric measurements.

lb. (pound), oz. (ounce), mi. (mile)
But: kg (kilogram), g (gram), km (kilometer), ml (milliliter)

Some objects, concepts, organizations, and businesses that are known popularly by their initials do not require periods.

> TV, CD (compact disc, certificate of deposit), CEO (chief executive officer), FYI (for your information), IBM, UN, PTA

Some words are abbreviated by reducing them to one or two initial syllables or to portions of one or more syllables. Use a period with those abbreviations.

> Amer. (America), arr. (arrive), min. (minute), lang. (language)

If an abbreviation comes at the end of a sentence, only one period is needed, not two.

> He is the president of Media Services, Inc.

A comma may be used after the period of an abbreviation.

> The U.S.A., India, and two other countries were at the UN conference, which lasted until 11 P.M.

If a period is used between letters in an abbreviation, no space is required after the period: *U.S.A.* However, a space may be used between two initials of a person's name: *J. G. McGraw.*

Names of days and months and units of measure should be spelled out when they occur in sentences.

---

13 Use periods where they are necessary with the following abbreviations.
- Address
  Mr M T Feller, C E O
  E A Crane Co
  203 N Fourth St
  St Paul, Minn 55108 U S A

- Itinerary
  Dept time: Mon, Jan 31, 3:35 P M ; Tokyo, Jpn
  Arr time (approx): Tues, Feb 1, 6:40 A M ; Helsinki, Fin

- Ingredients
  ~~butter 200 g   flour 500 ml   sugar 350 g~~

- Class Schedule
  first hr : chem ; second hr : econ
  third hr : Ger ; fourth hr : anthrop

EXCLAMATION POINT

Use an exclamation point at the end of a sentence to express surprise, disbelief, or other strong emotion.

An exclamation point may be used in place of a question mark when an emotion such as surprise or anger is being expressed.

> You what! You had an accident with my car!

Sometimes exclamation points are used to give very strong warnings or to make demands, commands, or very strong requests.

> Opening this door will sound an alarm! Absolutely no parking here! Do it now! Don't forget it again!

An exclamation point may be used for emphasis or to help clarify a point in a sentence.

> I said fifty, not fifteen!

Exclamation points can be very strong, and they are not often necessary. A period or a comma may not be used with an exclamation point.

---

14 Punctuate the following with exclamation points or periods.
- Slow down We're too close to that car
- Please don't drive so fast
- Watch out Don't ever try that again
- We can't park here This is a bus stop
- You can let me off at the next corner

CAPITALIZATION 3

Titles of songs, films, software, and books and other publications are capitalized. The first word, the last word, and the main words of titles are always capitalized, including all nouns, pronouns, verbs, adjectives, and adverbs. It is not necessary to capitalize articles (*a, an, the*) or conjunctions (*and, or, nor, but, for*) or prepositions (*in, of, to, on*) that have fewer than four letters, unless they are the first or last words of a title. Figures should not be used in titles; numbers are spelled out.

Tender Is the Night   One Flew Over the Cuckoo's Nest

When an article is the first word in the title of a newspaper or similar publication, the article is not capitalized when the title of the publication appears in a sentence.

The New York Times
I was busy all day Sunday reading the *New York Times*.

---

15 Circle the letters of any words in the following titles that should not be capitalized.
- *How To Prepare For Exams*
- *A Guide To The Metropolitan Museum*
- *Be My Love*
- *Don't Look Behind You*
- *A Study Of The Present Tense*
- *Just Between You And Me*

Part Two

COMMA 5

A comma is usually not necessary after brief expressions of time or place at the beginning of a sentence. (See also transitional expressions of chronology in Comma 6.)

> Yesterday afternoon I went to the festival with my friends.
> At the festival I saw my boss and his wife.

A comma may be helpful to a reader when the expression of time or place is long; however, long expressions of time or place usually read more smoothly when they follow or come within the main clause.

> Tomorrow at around two o'clock, I'll be at the festival.
> *Better:* I'll be at the festival tomorrow at around two o'clock.
> In the shop across from the festival grounds, I saw Maria.
> *Better:* I saw Maria in the shop across from the festival grounds.

Use a comma with an expression of time or place, or reword a sentence, when the sentence might be awkward to read without a comma.

> At the festival, crowds were quite thick by lunchtime.
> *Better:* Crowds were quite thick at the festival by lunchtime.
> In the afternoon, performances in the stadium were delayed.
> *Better:* Performances in the stadium were delayed in
>   the afternoon.

16 Use commas where necessary in the following sentences, or reword them to make their meaning clear.

- At eleven o'clock buses stopped running in this part of town.
- Last year there was a transportation strike here too.
- In today's newspaper there's an article about the strike.
- At the top of the page one of the bus drivers is interviewed.
- At the taxi company drivers are working overtime.
- By tomorrow the bus strike will probably be over.

QUESTION MARK 2

Question words and question word order do not always indicate the need for a question mark. The following are not questions, and they should not be punctuated with a question mark.

> Will you please close the window. *polite request*
> What a beautiful day! *exclamation*
> "How I Spent My Weekend" *adverbial phrase*
> I'd like to know if we are going to have a test. *embedded question*
> I wonder how much longer she'll be here. *embedded question*
> She asked me when the summer vacation began. *embedded question*

17 Use a question mark or a period to end the following sentences.

- I asked our guide about our itinerary
- Did he say anything about where we were going to have lunch
- You're going to the museum with us, aren't you
- The guide lent me his book *How to Enjoy Europe on a Small Budget*
- I also recommend *Are You Ready to Go Abroad*
- Have you read *How to Study a Foreign Language*

APOSTROPHE 3

An apostrophe is used with the plural of letters when they are referred to as letters of the alphabet. (See also Italics.)

> I got three *A*'s on my report card.
> My name is spelled with two *t*'s, not one.
> Are these *m*'s or *n*'s?

An apostrophe is not necessary with the plural form of an abbreviation unless an apostrophe would contribute to clarity as, for example, when the period of an abbreviation comes before the *-s* suffix.

> The PTAs from several schools met last night.
> When I graduate in June, I will have two Ph.D.'s.

No apostrophe is necessary when an *-s* is used to indicate more than one such word.

> You typed two *and*s in this sentence.
> The *of*s should not be capitalized in the title.

An apostrophe is not necessary with the plural of numbers as figures, nor is an apostrophe used with the plural of spelled-out numbers.

> the 1900s   hundreds of people
> I gave her two 50s, and she gave me ten 10s
>   (monetary currency).
> Tens of thousands of people watched the game on TV.

---

18 Review Apostrophe 1 and 2, and then punctuate the following with apostrophes where they are necessary.

- Yesterdays picnic wasnt much fun.
- The temperature was in the 30s, and it was a very wet and windy day.
- We werent able to start a fire to cook anything.
- We had some salad, but we couldnt barbecue the chicken.
- We couldnt drink any juice because we didnt have any cups.
- We sat in T. J.s car and played some games and listened to our new CDs.

COMMA 6

A comma may be used with transitional expressions of chronology, such as *finally, first, first of all, lastly, last of all, next, second,* and *secondly.* A comma is not necessary after *then* when it expresses chronology. (See also Comma 3 on the use of commas with introductory words and phrases, and Comma 8 on commas with other transitional expressions.)

> My schedule is almost the same every morning. First, I usually jog around the neighborhood or do some exercise in my room. Second, I take a shower. Next, I eat some toast and an egg for breakfast. Then I listen to the morning news or read the newspaper, and finally, I leave for school.

19 Use commas where they are necessary in the following two paragraphs.

There are several reasons why I have decided to move out of the college dormitory and look for an apartment. First of all my room is very small. I don't even have room for my new computer desk. Secondly the dormitory is very noisy in the evening and I find it difficult to study there. Lastly the college recently increased the dormitory fee. I am sure I can find a quiet and inexpensive apartment not too far from the campus.

Today was a very busy day for me. First my friends gathered at my dormitory room at around 8 A.M. Then we packed all of my things into several boxes. Next we put the boxes into my friends' cars and after that we drove to my new apartment. Then we unloaded the cars unpacked the boxes and put away all of my things. Finally I made some pizza for my friends and we sat around and watched television for a while.

COMMA 7

Use a comma when a dependent clause comes before an independent clause. Dependent clauses often begin with *after, before, since, until, when, whenever, while* (expressions of time); *where, wherever,* (expressions of place); *as, as if, as long as, as though, because, since* (expressions of cause or reason); *in order that, so that* (expressions of purpose or result); and *although, even though, if, provided that, though,* and *unless* (expressions of concession and condition).

> Because I have a test tomorrow, I can't watch the
> World Cup on TV.
> If your favorite team loses the game, don't get upset.
> After we watch the game, we're planning to have
> dinner together.

It is not necessary to use a comma between clauses when an independent clause comes before a dependent clause.

> I can't watch the World Cup on TV because I have a
> test tomorrow.
> Don't get upset if your team loses the game.
> We're planning to have dinner together after we watch
> the game.

---

20 **Use commas where necessary in the following sentences.**
- If you leave now you'll be on time.
- As soon as you get to the airport give me a call.
- Get something for Ken at the souvenir shop if you have time.
- Even if you don't have time you'd better get something for Ken.
- I can't take you to the airport because I am busy this afternoon.
- Although I can't take you to the airport I can pick you up when you come back.

SEMICOLON 1

A semicolon may be used in place of a period to end the first sentence in a pair of related sentences. This use of the semicolon expresses or establishes a close relationship between the pair of sentences. Sometimes a semicolon suggests *and, but, for, nor, or, yet, so,* or *because,* but not always. The second sentence in a pair of sentences separated by a semicolon often adds more information to or clarifies the first sentence. A sentence following a semicolon is not capitalized.

> I wouldn't take the freeway; they are doing repair work on it.
> Don't turn left at the corner; turn right.
> I need to get some gas; let's stop here.

A period can be used in place of a semicolon in the previous and following ~~examples; however, a semicolon links the sentences more strongly.~~ A comma cannot be used in place of a semicolon in the examples.

> I haven't seen Stella in a long time; I'm going to give her a call.
> I'll go and get my books and things; you wait here for Martin.

---

21 Rewrite the following sentences replacing the commas and conjunctions with semicolons.

- Math is easy for my friends, but it's difficult for me.
- I like our math teacher, but I don't care for the class.
- History is my best subject, and economics is my worst.
- I'm studying Chinese because I want to become an expert on the Far East.
- Foreign languages are easy for me, so I think I'll work for the UN.
- Speaking Chinese is fairly easy, but reading it is difficult.

22 Punctuate the following with semicolons.

- My friend thought the movie was terrific I thought it was boring.
- I really don't care to see films with a lot of violence I don't like musicals either.
- I like to go to movies I never watch them on TV.
- I don't go to movies often they are expensive, and I am on a tight budget.
- Nobody likes the theater near the campus the seats are very uncomfortable.
- I don't know whether I'll go to a movie next weekend maybe I'll stay home and study.

SEMICOLON 2; COMMA 8

Transitional expressions are used to make two related sentences read smoothly together. Common transitional expressions include *accordingly, also, besides, consequently, finally, for example, furthermore, however, in addition, in contrast, moreover, nevertheless, on the other hand, otherwise, similarly, therefore,* and *unfortunately.* In the examples below, the first independent clause may be punctuated with a period or a semicolon. A transitional expression is followed by a comma.

> I couldn't find my favorite recipe; therefore, I had to make the pie from memory.
> The pie is still hot; otherwise, I would offer you some.
> I baked the pie too long; however, it doesn't taste bad.
> I enjoy cooking; in fact, I sometimes think I should have been a cook.
> The kitchen is a mess; nevertheless, I'm not going to clean it up until I've had a chance to sit down for a while.

Some transitional expressions may also come after a comma at the end of a sentence or independent clause. These expressions include *however, nevertheless,* and *otherwise.*

> Microwave ovens are very convenient; they are not recommended for baking bread, however.
> The pie is still hot; I would offer you some, otherwise.
> The kitchen is very messy; I'm not going to clean it up just now, nevertheless.

Accordingly, consequently, furthermore, however, in contrast, moreover, nevertheless, on the other hand, otherwise, therefore, and *unfortunately* may occur within a sentence; this word order, however, is more typical of formal written English. When a transitional expression occurs within a sentence, it is set off with commas and generally precedes the main verb.

> Microwave ovens are very convenient; they are not, however, recommended for baking bread.
> The kitchen is a terrible mess; I am, nevertheless, not going to clean it up just now.

I like apple pie; my wife, on the other hand, prefers
cheesecake.

I couldn't find the recipe; I, therefore, had to make the pie
from memory.

Some of the introductory words and expressions that were introduced in
Comma 3 may also be punctuated like the examples above.

I like to make desserts; in fact, they are the only thing I like
to make.

I'm afraid I don't care for any ice cream; actually, I'm on a diet.

When a period is used in place of a semicolon to end a sentence, the first
word of the following sentence is always capitalized.

My wife likes to make cheesecake; however, she always turns
down desserts.

Or: My wife likes to make cheesecake. However, she always
turns down desserts.

23 Punctuate the following with semicolons and commas.
- We have some cinnamon in the cupboard it is very old however.
- This recipe is my grandmother's therefore it should be very good.
- We don't have any tea consequently I can't offer you any.
- This coffee is very weak moreover it is almost cold.
- I've already had two pieces of pie I'll have another small
piece nevertheless.
- I've eaten too much I am therefore going to skip dinner.

**24 Write out the following using commas and semicolons where they are
appropriate.**
- Fish is low in fat and it is high in protein.
- Fresh fish is difficult to get in this part of the country I would eat
more of it otherwise.
- Have some fried carrots or eat one raw as a snack.
- Actually I like vegetables I do not eat a lot of fruit however.
- Celery is an excellent food but too much of it is not good for you.
- I usually avoid greasy foods nevertheless I sometimes have french
fries with a hamburger.

COMMA 9

Steve and *the violin* in the sentences below are examples of **nonrestrictive appositives**; that is, the appositives are unessential, and the basic meaning of the sentences stays the same if the appositives are removed. Nonrestrictive appositives are set off with commas.

> Carla and her brother, Steve, have a lot in common.
> Both of them play a musical instrument, the violin.

A **restrictive appositive** is information that is part of the word or words that it modifies. In the first example below, the restrictive appositive, *Elizabeth*, provides essential information; it tells which of Carla's sisters likes jazz. This is in contrast to the nonrestrictive appositive in the example above, from which we learn that Carla has only one brother, Steve. The identity of the opera is essential information in the second example, so *The Magic Flute* is also a restrictive appositive. Restrictive appositives are not set off with commas.

> Carla's sister Elizabeth likes jazz.
> Mozart's opera *The Magic Flute* is Carla's favorite.

Relative clauses are also restrictive or nonrestrictive. The first example below contains a nonrestrictive relative clause, and the second example contains a restrictive relative clause.

> Carla, who started lessons when she was four, has been
>   studying the violin for 12 years.
> The teacher who composed this symphony is Carla's teacher.

In the following example, *in the front of the class* is a reduced restrictive relative clause. Commas are not used in this case.

> The student in the front of the class is Carla.

25 Use commas to set off any nonrestrictive appositives in the following sentences.

- The conductor of the orchestra Rochus Feller is a good friend of Carla and Steve's parents.
- Rochus Feller's brother is Martin Feller the famous cellist.
- The Toronto Symphony Orchestra violinist Anna-Marie Hatano is related to Martin Feller.
- Carla and Steve's father has written one piece of music a violin concerto.
- The Juilliard school one of the most famous music schools in the country is where Steve and Carla's parents met.
- The Austrian composer Mozart is Carla's favorite.

26 Use commas to set off any nonrestrictive relative clauses in the following sentences.

- Our new music hall which was completed in May is already famous overseas.
- The person who designed the hall is Steve and Carla's uncle.
- Their uncle who is only 29 years old is well known for his work.
- The building across from the music hall is the old public library.
- The library a white marble building is a popular tourist attraction.
- People who have attended concerts in the new hall say that it is very comfortable.

COLON 1

A colon is often used to introduce and to give special attention or emphasis to a series of items; however, a sentence may be reworded so that a colon is not necessary.

> There are only three countries in Africa that I have never visited: Nigeria, Ghana, and Liberia.
> Or: Nigeria, Ghana, and Liberia are the only countries in Africa that I have never visited.

A colon may introduce more than one independent clause or other long element. The first word of a sentence or other element after a colon does not have to be capitalized. (See also Semicolon 3.)

> Our teacher has made three rules for us: don't be late for class; leave class quietly; and always bring a notebook and pen to class.

A long sentence or more than one related sentence following a colon may be capitalized.

> Not all of my friends live in the dormitory: A few live with their families. Others have apartments.

A colon may also be used to introduce an appositive.

> Most people in Egypt speak the same language: Arabic.
> The longest river in the world runs through Egypt: the Nile.

The following expressions, followed by a comma, may be preceded by a colon or a semicolon: *for example*, *namely*, *specifically*, and *that is*.

> We stopped in three countries on our way to Egypt: namely, Algeria, Morocco, and Libya.
> Let's spend another night in Cairo; that is, if you don't mind.

---

27 Use commas and colons where they are appropriate in the following sentences.

- I'd like to have Indian or North African food for lunch.
- Two restaurants near the campus serve North African dishes the Cairo House and the Marrakesh.
- Jorge Peter Anna and I had dinner at the Marrakesh last week.
- The Marrakesh is closed three days each week Sundays Mondays and Tuesdays.
- The Cairo House restaurant has very good food but it's rather expensive.
- There are two things that the Cairo House is famous for namely coffee and Egyptian bread.

COMMA 10

Use a comma before a tag question and after *yes* and *no* in sentences that are replies to questions.

> You haven't seen my bicycle, have you? No, I haven't.
> You're coming in my car, right? Yes, if that's OK.

---

28 Use commas, question marks, and periods where they are required in the following sentences.
- You came by car didn't you   No I came by bus
- You'll be getting a ride won't you   Yes I think so
- Grace usually comes to school on her bicycle doesn't she
  Yes usually
- You don't need a ride tomorrow do you   No that's OK
- You wanted to borrow my car tonight isn't that right   Yes is
  that OK

SEMICOLON 3

Use a semicolon instead of a comma with a series of items when the items include commas.

> There were only five people at the meeting: Martin, a professional basketball player; Dan, Martin's coach; Henry, Martin's lawyer; and Martin's brother, Rochus.

Use a semicolon to separate long elements in a series.

> Yesterday was really busy. I met with my staff in the morning; I gave a speech at the club at lunchtime; and I was interviewed on TV for the Sunday evening news.

29 Punctuate the following with semicolons; also, use commas where they are necessary.

- On Monday morning I went to the dentist on Monday afternoon I went to the bank and Monday evening I made three long-distance calls to Mexico.
- On Wednesday one of my busiest days this month I had four difficult classes I practiced for two hours with the basketball team and I tutored my roommate in math for one hour.
- On Thursday I arranged basketball games for our team on Friday the fourth on Monday the seventh and on Thursday the tenth.
- On Friday my brother called me from São Paulo my sister called me from Rome and I got a birthday card from a friend in Kyoto.
- On Saturday I slept late I prepared for the marathon and I finished the work I started last month.
- On Sunday the day I usually spend relaxing I had calls from Tokyo Japan Paris France Lagos Nigeria and Vietnam.

Part Three

COMMA 11

Use a comma between adjectives if each adjective modifies a noun in the same manner.

> *Comma required:* a large, red coat (the coat is large and red)
> *Comma not required:* a large winter coat (the winter coat is large)
> *Comma required:* a difficult, boring class (the class is difficult and boring)
> *Comma not required:* a difficult Russian class (the Russian class is difficult)

A comma is not necessary after *very* or the expression *brand-new*, or after intensifiers ending in *-ly*, such as *incredibly* and *terribly*.

> a very large, empty house
> a brand-new pair of sunglasses
> a terribly cold day

30 Use commas where necessary in the following.
- an unusually heavy suitcase
- a large red and yellow leaf
- a sick baby elephant
- a long difficult novel
- a very important business letter
- a soft old comfortable chair

31 Use commas where necessary in the following.
- ~~some beautiful delicate flowers~~
- an exciting children's program
- a complicated computer software program
- a brand-new expensive sports car
- many very interesting books and magazines
- few modern office buildings

COMMA 12

A comma is generally used after a prepositional phrase at the beginning of a sentence. Some prepositional phrases may begin with *because of, besides, by* + verb + *-ing, except for, in addition to, in spite of, with regard to,* and *without* + verb + *-ing.* (See also Comma 5.)

> In spite of my low salary, I was able to send my son
>   to the university.
> By not buying a new car, we saved a lot of money.

When a prepositional phrase comes at the end of a sentence, a comma is not necessary.

> I was able to send my son to the university in spite of
>   my low salary.
> We saved a lot of money by not buying a new car.

32 Commas are missing from some of the following sentences.
Punctuate the sentences with commas where they are needed.
- Because of the warm weather the snow was not very good.
- We enjoyed our ski trip in spite of the poor quality of the snow.
- In spite of the fact that we were all beginners no one got hurt.
- Except for Kay everyone wants to go skiing again next weekend.
- Kay wants to go bowling instead of skiing.
- Without skiing regularly no one can learn to do it well.

QUOTATION MARKS

Use double quotation marks (" ") for direct quotations. The first word of a quotation is usually capitalized, and periods and commas go inside the final quotation mark. A comma or a colon may separate a quotation from an introductory phrase; however, if the quote is very short, no punctuation is necessary. A comma usually separates a quotation from the part of the sentence that follows the quotation.

> She said: "No." *Or:* She said, "No." *Or:* She said "No."
> *Or:* "No," she said.

Semicolons and colons go outside the final or closing quotation mark. Dashes, exclamation points, and question marks go outside the final quotation mark unless they are part of the quotation.

> She said, "The test won't be easy"!
> *But:* "Stop!" he shouted.
> Did she say "No"? *But:* Her reply was "Why?"

Quotation marks are not necessary with indirect quotations.

> She said that he was very helpful.
> He told me that he enjoyed helping her.

Although the first word of a quotation is normally capitalized, it is not necessary to capitalize an incomplete quotation that is only a part of a sentence. A comma is usually not necessary with a partial quotation.

> She said that she was "sorry." He promised he would give me a job "with a very good salary."

Use single quotation marks (' ') within double quotation marks, or reword a sentence so that single quotation marks are not necessary.

> She said: "My mother said, 'Absolutely not.'"
> *Or:* She said her mother said, "Absolutely not."

Quotation marks are used with chapter titles and titles of articles or other units of writing in a newspaper, magazine, or other publication.

> My favorite poem is "The Hollow Men."
> I suggest you read "Delicious Rice" in *Cooking for One Person.*

Quotation marks are not required with block quotations. A quotation of more than four lines, but not more than one paragraph, should be set off from the rest of the page by indenting it on the left side, or on both the right and left sides, and by putting additional space between the quotation and the rest of the text on a page.

If a quotation consists of more than one paragraph from the same source, quotation marks are used at the beginning of each paragraph, but at the end of only the last paragraph.

33 Use quotation marks, periods, commas, colons, and question marks where necessary in the following sentences.
- I can't tell you what she said to me
- Did she say she was sorry
- She said Oh, sorry
- I thought she said Don't worry
- On the phone last night she said My mother said to apologize
- What did you say to her

34 Punctuate the following sentences with quotation marks, commas, colons, periods, and question marks where they are required.
- Have you read Martin's book *The Life of a Chameleon*
- Lars said he read it in one day
- If the book is at the library Anna said she'd read it
- Martin said he would be happy to sign the book for us
- The chapter Chameleons as Pets is very interesting
- Did you say Chameleons

COLON 2

Like semicolons, a colon may be used to signal that a closely related sentence follows or to make two related sentences read smoothly. (See also Colon 1.)

> Don't waste time: go straight home after school.
> I thought it was impossible: My math teacher gave me an A, and I got an A in English.

In these examples, a colon can be replaced by a semicolon; however, a colon establishes a stronger connection between the two sentences than a semicolon does. The connection between the two sentences in these pairs is weakened somewhat when a period is used instead of a colon or a semicolon.

---

35 Rewrite each line below using colons, semicolons, periods, question marks, or commas. Some words may need to be capitalized.

- We're going to lose the game our best player is in the hospital
- Armando is a school hero he scored ten points in the game
- You're really not interested in attending the football game tonight are you
- That's what I don't like about baseball the games last so long
- Listen to what I heard today our teacher has a black belt in karate
- I know why he doesn't play basketball he doesn't like the coach

HYPHEN 1

Use a hyphen to divide a word of more than one syllable that will not fit at the end of a line of words.

Words may only be divided between syllables pronounced distinctly.

> di-vide hy-phen to-day book-store
> dic-tion-ary Eng-lish an-ni-ver-sa-ry

The -*ing* suffix may usually be separated from the syllable that comes before it.

> go-ing putt-ing (to putt) study-ing spell-ing us-ing

Some words double the final consonant before adding -*ing*. These words may be separated between the double consonants, not immediately before the -*ing*.

> bat-ting hit-ting run-ning put-ting (to put)

If a syllable is only one letter, it may not be separated from the syllable that follows it. The following words may not be divided where indicated with a slash mark.

a/gain   e/ven   a/mong   u/niversity   o/pen   a/bout

A syllable of only one or two letters is not separated from the syllable that comes before it. This rule also applies to the past tense -ed and the comparative -er suffixes. Also, a syllable consisting of a consonant + -le is not separated from the syllable that it follows. The following words may not be divided in the places that are indicated with a slash mark.

luck/y   stud/y   want/ed   moth/er   writ/er   lone/ly
mov/ie   mer/cy   comforta/ble   peo/ple

Words that are spelled with a hyphen should be separated only at the hyphen when they do not fit at the end of a line of words.

east-northeast   twenty-four   non-Japanese
ex-student   web-footed

---

36 **Some of the following words may be divided when there is not room for the entire word at the end of a line. Use a slash mark (/) to indicate where a division may occur. Some of the words may be separated in more than one place; other words may not be divided.**

- a v e n u e   i t e m   e q u a l   a w k w a r d   i m p o s s i b l e   t e x t b o o k
- s l e e p i n g   f i t t i n g   c a r e d   e f f o r t   o p e n e d   a l w a y s
- r a d i o   s e l f - t a u g h t   t e a c h e r   c o m p u t e r   u n i v e r s i t y

HYPHEN 2

Use a hyphen with the numbers twenty-one through ninety-nine. When fractions are spelled out, their numerators and denominators are separated with a hyphen, unless the numerator or denominator already includes a hyphen.

twenty-one   one hundred forty-two   two-sixteenths
But: thirty-two sixteenths

Use a hyphen with the following prefixes: *self-*, *all-*, and *ex-* when it means "former."

self-made   All-Africa Conference   ex-student

When a prefix is used with a proper noun or with a number, a hyphen is required.

pro-Kennedy   pre-10th anniversary sale   anti-Marxist
the post-Stalin era

A compound modifier with a number requires a hyphen when it comes before a noun. Notice the use of the singular noun in the compound modifier with a number.

a three-story house   two three-month terms
a half-inch piece of wood   a two-word verb

When two or more words form one unit to modify a noun, the words are usually joined with a hyphen; however, when the first of two words that modify a noun is an adverb ending in *-ly,* the two words are not joined with a hyphen.

a well-known book   a hard-working man
a world-famous actor
But: an unusually beautiful day   a frequently
    misunderstood person

When a unit of two or more words follows the noun that the words modify, the modifiers are not hyphenated.

Hard-working students get good grades.
Our school has well-trained teachers.
But: My students are not hard working.
The teachers here are well trained.

Some compound words are hyphenated. Other compounds are separated, and others are written as one word. In general, there is a tendency to write compound words as a single word. A good dictionary should be referred to when there is any doubt about the spelling of a compound word.

mother-in-law   vice-president   great-grandmother
blue-green   half-baked   self-service   do-it-yourself
German-American
high school   oil well   seat belt   soda water
schoolteacher   bookstore   roommate   stomachache
cookbook   grandmother   worldwide   coffeepot   software

---

37 Put a slash mark (/) where a hyphen should be used with modifiers in the following sentences.

- Ali's new eight hundred dollar bicycle was stolen from his house last night.
- Someone entered a first floor window of Ali's house while Ali was at the gym playing basketball.
- A neighbor said the burglar was about 180 centimeters tall and was wearing a white and yellow sweater.
- Another neighbor said she saw a 180 centimeter tall, strange looking man walking around in front of Ali's house a few days ago.
- Fortunately, Ali found his bicycle on the school grounds today.
- Unfortunately, the badly damaged bicycle will be impossible to repair.

PARENTHESES

Parentheses are sometimes used to enclose additional information or a clarification; however, parentheses should, in general, be avoided. Sentences with parentheses often do not read smoothly, and sometimes the use of parentheses to include an afterthought or additional information suggests careless or hasty writing.

An abbreviated form may be introduced in parentheses immediately following its unabbreviated form. Once an abbreviation has been brought to the attention of the reader in this manner, it can be used alone later in the text.

> The Air Safety Board (A.B.A.) held an emergency meeting yesterday. Usually the A.B.A. meets only once a month.

DASH

A dash may be used to emphasize or single out one or more words in a sentence. Because a dash signifies a pause, it usually brings more attention to a word or phrase than the comma, period, semicolon, or colon that might be used in its place.

One use of a dash is to set off a nonrestrictive appositive. (See also Comma 9.) Note that there is no space before or after a dash. On the typewriter a dash is formed with two hyphens (--).

> My favorite actress—Anna-Marie Harper—has a degree from the University of Paris.
> She was recently in a remake of an old film—*Gone With the Wind*.

A dash may be used before a conjunction with two independent clauses.

> I saw the movie—and I read the book too.
> I'd like to go with you—but I don't want to see *Casablanca* again.

A dash may be used between an independent clause and a dependent clause, but a dash should not be used if a dependent clause precedes an independent clause.

> I'm going to the theater tonight—if I don't have any homework.
> *But:* If Anna-Marie Harper is not in the movie, I don't want to see it.

In the examples below, the dash replaces a colon or a semicolon, drawing attention to the element that follows the dash.

> There is only one actor whom I really like—Martin Tai.
> Kay doesn't like movies—she hasn't seen one in years.
> The music in the film was good—the acting was terrible.

Avoid the overuse of dashes. Because a dash introduces a pause, too many dashes in writing can reduce readability.

38 **Read each of the following sentences aloud. Then insert dashes where they may be appropriate, replacing commas, colons, and semicolons. Read the sentences aloud again—with a pause where a dash occurs.**

- I know you don't care for horror movies, but I do.
- Let's rent another video tomorrow, if you don't have anything better to do.
- *The Third Man,* which is my favorite film, is showing at the Grand next week.
- I highly recommend the Grand Theater; it's air-conditioned.
- Ken enjoyed the movie for only one reason: the scenes of Vienna.
- Marc goes to movies regularly; in fact, he sees a film at least twice a week.

ELLIPSIS POINTS

Three points or periods, with one space before and after each of them, are used to indicate that one or more words have been omitted from material being quoted or excerpted.

> *Original:* Washington High School, one of the oldest schools in our town, is named after Booker T. Washington, not George Washington.
> *Excerpt:* "Washington High School . . . is named after Booker T. Washington, not George Washington."

When the end of a sentence is omitted, a period or other punctuation is required before the three ellipsis points.

> *Original:* Last spring two hundred young men and women graduated from the school, and 63 percent of them went on to college.
> *Excerpt:* "Last spring two hundred young men and women graduated from the school. . . ."

When the end of one sentence and the beginning of the following sentence have been omitted, three ellipsis points are used without a period or other sentence punctuation.

> *Original:* The ambassador of France gave a speech at the school several years ago. The French ambassador made his speech when he visited the school in 1974.
> *Excerpt:* "The ambassador of France gave a speech at the school . . . in 1974."

A period and three ellipsis points may be used when the end portion of a sentence and one or more following sentences have been omitted from a quotation. The sentences that precede and follow the ellipsis points must be grammatically complete.

> *Original:* The school was completed in 1990, and students were accepted in autumn of that year. Only 89 students enrolled the first year, but now there are over a thousand students at the school. In only four years, the school became well known for its athletic program.
> *Excerpt:* "The school was completed in 1990. . . . In only four years, the school became well known for its athletic program."

39 Rewrite the following sentences, replacing the underlined portions and the commas with ellipsis points.

· Lincoln High School, <u>which was founded in 1895,</u> is the oldest school in the city.

· Several graduates of the school have become famous, <u>including one graduate who is now the mayor of the city.</u>

· At a recent graduation ceremony, the mayor spoke to the students <u>about high school education. He talked</u> about changes in high school education in the United States.

· The mayor also said that <u>he thought that</u> students had not changed <u>during the twenty-five years</u> since he attended Lincoln High School.

· The students enjoyed the mayor's speech <u>even though it went on for more than an hour.</u>

· After the ceremony the mayor joined the new graduates at a banquet <u>in a hotel near the campus.</u>

ITALICS

Italics are used with titles of publications, songs, films, and works of art. Titles of chapters, articles, and other units of writing in a publication are usually not italicized. On a typewriter and in handwriting, italics are indicated by underlining. When the first word of the title of a newspaper or similar publication is an article, the article is not italicized when the title appears within a sentence. (See also Capitalization 3.)

> *The New York Times*   *The Third Man*   *Mona Lisa*

Unfamiliar words from other languages are put in italics.

> There was no *natto* on the menu at the Kiku Restaurant.

Words that are referred to as words and letters referred to as letters of the alphabet are italicized.

> Be careful not to confuse *any way* with *anyway.*
> The plural of *book* is formed with an *-s.*

Words may sometimes be italicized for emphasis.

I said *glow*, not *grow*.
If you don't come to class on time, our teacher *really*
gets angry.

---

40 In the sentences below, underline any words that should be in italics.

- I sometimes find good recipes in the Sunday edition of
  the newspaper.
- The pie Jean made was just good; the pie Lorraine made was
  very good.
- I like Thai food, but I don't care for dom yam.
- Some of my favorite recipes are from the cookbook Recipes
  From Around the World.
- There is a good recipe for pizza in the chapter on Italian food.
- I'm still not used to using the metric system in recipes.

NUMBERS

In technical writing and in tables and graphs, figures may be used;
however, except for indicating page numbers or reporting scores or
similar kinds of information, the numbers one through ten and numbers
that begin a sentence should always be spelled out in ordinary writing.
Figures may be used for numbers 11 through 100, and larger numbers
should be spelled out if they are not more than two words. Hyphenated
numbers are considered as one word. The guide for using figures
and writing out numbers also applies to ordinal numbers.

page 50   99 percent   seven hundred   354,000
the first ten pages   our 25th wedding anniversary

Amounts of more than a million may be written as a combination of figures and spelled out numbers. This applies also to amounts of money involving more than a million units. Smaller amounts of money may be written out if they do not include two units of money, such as dollars and cents. A monetary symbol, such as a dollar sign, may accompany figures, but if an amount of money is written out, the name for the unit of money should also be spelled out.

> $5.95   The population is now 135 million.
> sixty-six billion yen $42 billion

Figures are used with dates; however, dates should not be expressed with virgules or hyphens, as in 10/25/94 or 10-25-94. References to a particular century are spelled out.

> 10 February 1995   January 23, 1919   the twenty-first century

The time of day is always spelled out when it is used with *o'clock*, and it may be spelled out to indicate whole hours and periods of a quarter of an hour and a half hour. Figures are used with A.M. and P.M. and when reference is made to a scheduled time. Lowercase a.m. and p.m. may also be used to refer to the time of day.

> nine o'clock   a quarter after seven   four-thirty in the morning
> 10 P.M.   6:26   7:10 in the morning

41 In the following sentences, write out the numbers that should be words instead of numerals.

- 2 of the city's 3 lakes are near my apartment.
- My neighborhood is only 12 miles from the airport, or about 45 minutes by car.
- The population of the city, which is 289,651, has decreased by .3 percent over the past 24 months.
- Recently more than $18,000,000,000 has been spent on a new subway system here.
- The basic fare for the subway is $2.00.
- A ceremony to inaugurate the new subway will be held at 9:00 A.M. on June 3.

Appendix

PUNCTUATION IN BIBLIOGRAPHIES

Notice the use of periods, commas, quotation marks, colons, italics or underlining, and the formats for footnotes and bibliographies below.

Format for books:
Family name, given name. Book title underlined or in italics. Place of publication: Publisher, year of publication.

> Voeller, Edward. The Red-Crowned Crane. Minneapolis: Dillon Press, Inc., 1989.

Format for articles:
Family name, given name. "Article title in double quotation marks." Title of publication underlined or in italics, Date of publication, page numbers of the article.

> Curtsinger, Bill. "Close Encounters with the Gray Reef Shark." National Geographic, January 1995, pp. 45–67.

PUNCTUATION IN LETTERS

Notice the use of periods, commas, and other punctuation in the return address heading, the inside address, the salutation, and the closing in correspondence.

The return address includes the sender's address and the date, but not the sender's name:

> 1146 Green Street
> St. Paul, Minnesota 55000
>
> January 16, 1997

1146 Green Street
St. Paul, Minnesota 55000

January 16, 1997

Return address

John Harper
Managing Editor
The Student News
945 Alvin Street
St. Paul, Minnesota 55000

Inside address

Salutation

Dear Mr. Harper,
I am writing to introduce myself and to inquire about employment opportunities at the Student News.

I am in my fourth year at Lincoln High School, and I am interested in part-time or freelance work as a photographer at your magazine. Currently, I am a member of the staff of the student newspaper at school, and I want to make a career in photojournalism.

My grade point average at Lincoln is 3.8, and I have applied for Western University beginning next year. Work taking pictures for the Student News would help me save for my university education, and it would provide very valuable experience.

I am enclosing a resume and two photographs as samples of my work. I will be giving you a call within a week with the hope that I can set up an appointment to meet with you.

Closing

Sincerely yours,

Arthur Gerard

Arthur Gerard

Enclosures

The inside address includes the name and the address of the person to whom the letter is addressed.

> John Harper
> Managing Editor
> The Student News
> 945 Alvin Street
> St. Paul, Minnesota 55000

A comma or, more formally, a colon is used with the salutation.

> Dear Mr. Harper, Dear Ms Keller: Dear Sir or Madam:

The closing is punctuated with a comma.

> Sincerely yours, Or: Sincerely, Or: Cordially,

SPELLING RULES

Although spelling rules contain many exceptions, the following guides are often helpful for writing words accurately. Always consult a dictionary when there is any doubt about the spelling of a word.

NOUN PLURAL FORMS

Add -s to most words to form the plural; form the plural of most words that end in -s, -z, -sh, -ch, or -x by adding -es.

> Add -s: book → books Add -es: church → churches

Words that end in -y:

If the letter before the -y is a consonant, change the -y to -ie and add -s. If the letter before the -y is a, e, i, o, or u, add -s to the -y. If the word ending in -y is a proper name, -s is usually added to the -y.

> Change -y to -ie and add -s: city → cities   penny → pennies
> french fry → french fries
> Add -s to -y: boy → boys   day → days   the Kennedys

Words that end in -o:

If a vowel comes before the -*o*, the plural is usually formed by adding -*s*. If the -*o* is preceded by a consonant, -*es* is usually added to form the plural. A few words ending in a consonant + -*o* may form the plural by adding -*s* or -*es*.

Add -*s:* stereo → stereos   rodeo → rodeos
Add -*es:* potato → potatoes   hero → heroes
Exceptions: photo → photos   piano → pianos
Add -*s* or -*es:* tornado → tornados or tornadoes

OTHER SUFFIXES

Noun suffixes -ence, -ance:

Verbs that take the -*ence* suffix to form a noun usually change their pattern of stress after the suffix is added.

prefer → preference   refer → reference

Verbs that take the -*ance* suffix usually do not change their pattern of stress.

rely → reliance   perform → performance

Nouns that do not originate from a verb usually take the -*ence* suffix.

intelligence   sentence

Adding suffixes to words that end in -e:

To add a suffix to a word that ends with an -*e*, drop the final -*e* if the suffix begins with a vowel.

surprise + -*ing:* surprising   rule + -*ed:* ruled
Exceptions: change → changing, *but:* changeable
mile → mileage

The final -*e* of a word usually is not dropped if the suffix begins with a consonant.

move + -*ment:* movement

The suffix -*ful* has only one *l*.

awful   beautiful   cheerful   spoonful

DOUBLING CONSONANTS

If a word has only one syllable and the word ends with a single vowel + a consonant, the final consonant is repeated before adding *-ing, -ed, -er, -est*, or other suffixes that begin with a vowel.

flip → flipper   hot → hottest   win → winning   beg → begged
Exception: bus → busing

If a word consists of more than one syllable, and if it ends in a single vowel + a consonant, the final consonant is doubled if the stress on the final syllable does not shift or change when the suffix is added to the word.

begin → beginner   omit → omitted   control → controlling

In the following example, the final stress changes, so the final consonant is not doubled.

confer → conference

If the final syllable of a word is not stressed, the final consonant is not doubled.

enter → entering   color → colored

RULES FOR *-IE* AND *-EI*

Frequently, *-i* comes before *-e* in a word. After the letter *-c*, *-ei* is more common than *-ie*. Also, *-ei* sometimes represents the *ay* sound as in *eight*, *weight*, and *freight*. Unfortunately, there are many exceptions to these guides.

-i before *-e:* chief   die   lie
after the letter *-c:* receive   receipt
an [ay] sound: freight   sleigh
Exceptions: foreign   height   either   science   being

WORDS IN FOCUS

The words in the list below are sometimes confusing for both beginning and experienced writers.

a, an: It is the first sound, not the first letter, of a word that decides which indefinite article may precede a word; use *a* before a consonant sound and *an* before a vowel sound. **Examples:** an *m*, an *s*, a *u*. *An* should be used before *m* and *s* when they are referred to as letters because, although they represent consonants, these letters begin with vowel sounds. The article *a* should be used before the letter *u* as a letter because the first sound of that letter is a consonant sound. **Additional examples:** *a university, an unusual person, a history, an hour.*

accept, except: *Accept* means "to receive something"; *except* means "to leave out" or "exclude." **Examples:** *Ken has been accepted at three universities. He does well in every subject except chemistry.*

a couple, a couple of: These expressions may be used in speech, but in writing, *a few, several,* or *two* is more appropriate.

affect, effect: *Affect* is usually a verb, and *effect* is usually a noun. **Examples:** *How did the dry weather affect your tomato plants? The dry weather had a bad effect on the tomato plants. Effect* is sometimes used as a verb as in the expression *to effect a change,* which means "to bring about a change."

all ready, already: *All ready* means "prepared," and *already* is used to express the idea of the completion of something. **Examples:** *Everything is all ready for the party. I've already seen this movie two times.*

all right, alright: *Alright* is a common misspelling of *all right.*

allude, elude: *Allude,* which is usually followed by *to,* means "to refer to indirectly." *Elude* means "to escape" or "to avoid." **Examples:** *When I asked him about school, he thought I was alluding to his poor grade in math. Eluding responsibility is a sign of cowardice.*

alphabetization: There are two systems for ordering words alphabetically in a list when an item on the list consists of more than one word. In the **letter-by-letter system**, the spaces between words are ignored, and each letter of all the words in an item is considered, up to the point where there is a period, comma, colon, or semicolon. In the **word-by-word system**, the first word of each of the items in a list is first considered; then the second word is alphabetized; and so on. In the letter-by-letter system, *a couple* comes after *accept*, and in the word-by-word system *a couple* precedes *accept*. This book uses the letter-by-letter system, though there are advantages to each method.

among, between: In general, *between* is used to refer to two items, and *among* is used with more than two. **Examples:** *There was very little space between the two cars. Among all the cars in the showroom, the red sports car is my favorite.*

any more, anymore: *Any more* (after *not*) means "to have no more"; *anymore* means "no longer." **Examples:** *I spent all my money. I don't have any more. I don't have any money in the bank anymore.*

anyplace: *Anyplace* is acceptable in speech, but *anywhere* should be used in writing.

anyway: The correct form is *anyway*, never *anyways*.

as, like: *Like* is a preposition; *as* is a conjunction that can join two clauses. **Examples:** *March in Chicago is like January in Tokyo. The novel ended as I had expected. As*, of course, is also used in comparisons. **Example:** *It's as light as a feather.*

a while, awhile: These two expressions are used differently, but they are the same in meaning. *Awhile* is an adverb; *a while* is an article + a noun, and it requires the preposition *for*. **Examples:** *I'll be outside awhile. I'll be outside for a while.*

beside, besides: *Beside* is used to indicate place or position; *besides* means "in addition to." **Examples:** *He stood beside the president. Besides Chinese, he also speaks Swahili.*

between: *Between* requires an object pronoun. **Example:** *Between you and me.* Not: *Between you and I.* See also *among, between*.

bring, take: One *brings* something toward someone or something and *takes* something away from someone or something.

can't hardly: The correct form is *can hardly.*

center, centre: *Center* is the American spelling, and *centre* is British. Many other words are spelled (the past form *spelt* is more common in British English) differently by the Americans and the British, and a few are indicated in the examples below. In the following pairs of words, the first spelling should be used for American readers: *color, colour; theater, theatre; installment, instalment; program, programme.* In addition, American writers usually use a *z* in some words where British writers often use an *s*: *alphabetize, alphabetise; recognize, recognise.* Writers of British English may also divide words at the end of a line differently from the accepted custom among American writers.

compare to, compare with: Either expression may be used to talk about similarities or differences.

complement, compliment: *Compliment,* as a verb or a noun, means "to praise someone." The verb *complement* means "to go well with." **Example:** *That hat complements your jacket, and that is a compliment.*

conscience, conscious: A *conscience* is the feeling people have for what is right to do and what is wrong to do, what is moral and immoral. To be *conscious* means "to be aware of what is going on" or "to be awake."

data: *Data* is the plural form of the Latin word *datum,* and *data* must be used with a plural verb form. **Example:** *These data are very old.* The words *criteria* and *media* are also plural forms of nouns. The singular forms are *criterion* and *medium.*

decent, descent: *Decent* is an adjective that often means "appropriate," "acceptable," or "nice." *Descent* is a noun that is often used in discussions about ancestry.

dessert, desert: A *desert* is one of the dry, sandy areas of the world where there are few plants; a *dessert* is sometimes served after a meal.

different from, different than: *Different from* is the more correct form. However, *different than* is often used in conversation and in cases where *different from* may be awkward.

economic, economical: *Economic* usually refers to the subject of economics. *Economical* means "money-saving" or "thrifty."

especially, specially: *Especially* means "particularly"; *specially* means "for a specific purpose." **Examples:** *I like dogs, especially boxers. This is a specially designed car.*

etc.: This abbreviation for two Latin words should be avoided in ordinary writing. Use *and so on* or *and other* + noun or a similar expression. **Example:** *We visited the zoo, the art museum, and other sights in the city.* Not: *We visited the zoo, the museum, etc.*

everyday, every day: *Everyday* is an adjective. To refer to something that happens daily, use *every day.* **Examples:** *I work out at the gym every day. Jogging is not an everyday activity for me.*

everyone, every one: *Everyone* is a pronoun used to refer to all persons. *One* is also a pronoun, and it can be used to refer to people, animals, or things. *Every one* is similar to saying *each one.*

farther, further: Use *farther* for distance between two points; *further* is used to refer to something that takes time or to express an additional amount of time. **Example:** *I need to study the map a little further before we go any farther.*

feel bad, feel good: *Feel bad* and *feel good* may be used to describe a physical or emotional condition. *Feel well* is considered acceptable, but *feel good* should be used with *about. Badly* may be used as an adverb to describe a result or an effect. **Examples:** *I don't feel bad about my English test. I didn't do too badly on it. I don't, however, feel very good about failing my chemistry class.*

fewer, less: *Fewer* is used with countable nouns, and *less* is used with uncountable nouns. **Examples:** *fewer classes, fewer tests; less time, less help.*

have got: To express possession, use *have* with *got*, never *got* alone. The verb *got (get)* means "received." **Example:** *I got your message, and yes, I've got your tennis racket.*

historic, historical: *Historic* means "important" or "something that will be remembered." *Historical* has to do with history.

house, home: A *house* is a structure. A *home* is a broader term and often includes the notion of livability or family life and the pleasantness associated with it.

into, in to: *Into* is always used to indicate direction or place; *in to* occurs when it precedes a verb. **Examples:** *He drove into a tree. I stopped in to see my teacher.*

kind of: *Kind of,* when used to mean "rather" or "somewhat," should be avoided in writing. **Example:** *The test was rather difficult.* Not: *kind of difficult.*

lay, lie: *Lay (lay, laid, laid)* means "to put something down" or "spread something out," and *lay* requires a direct object. *Lie (lie, lay, lain)* is what a person does on a flat surface. **Examples:** *I always lie in bed for an hour after I wake up. Let's lay the blankets on the bed.*

lend, loan: In writing, use *loan* as a noun and *lend* as a verb.

loose, lose: *Loose* is the opposite of *tight; lose* means "misplace."

maybe, may be: *Maybe* is an adverb that means "perhaps." The verb *may* is often combined with *be* to express possibility. **Example:** *We may be late for our appointment.*

precede, proceed: *Precede* means "to come before." *Proceed* means "to go ahead."

pretty: Use *rather* or *somewhat,* not *pretty,* to modify a word in written English. **Example:** *This is a rather difficult test.* Not: *This is a pretty difficult test.*

really: Use *really* before adjectives in speech, but not in writing. **Example:** *It's very nice.* Not: *It's really nice.*

rise, raise: An object is required with *raise;* no object is required with *rise.* **Examples:** *Raise your hand if you agree. If you agree, please rise.*

shall: *Shall* is used very little in American English except in questions with *I* and *we.* **Examples:** *Shall I meet you at the corner? What time shall we meet?*

sight, site, cite: A *sight* is something that is seen, and a *site* is a specific spot or location. **Examples:** *There are a lot of historical sights in Prague. The site of the new airport is only 40 minutes from downtown. Cite* is a verb that means "to show proof" or "to show an example" or, in legal terms, "to officially accuse someone of a crime."

sit, set: *Sit* refers to a position a person takes on a chair. *Set* means "to put something down." *Sit* does not require an object, but *set* does. **Examples:** *Sit on the chair. Set these things on the chair.*

sometime, some time: *Sometime* refers to a time in the future. *Some time* is an amount of time. **Example:** *Sometime on Saturday I'll spend some time working on the car.*

stationary, stationery: *Stationary*, with an *a*, means "not movable." *Stationery*, with an *e*, means "writing paper." As a memory aid, think of the *e* in *letter*, and write *stationery*.

supposed to: *Supposed to* is the correct form, not *suppose to*. **Example:** *We are supposed to be at the airport at 4:30.*

till, until: Both of these words are acceptable; however, *until* seems to be preferred. The form *'til* should not be used in formal writing.

too + adj. + a/an + noun: *It's too expensive a car.* Not: *It's too expensive of a car. Of* is not necessary in this expression.

toward, towards: Although both of these words are acceptable, *toward* is preferred.

turn around, turn round: Both expressions are acceptable, but in American English *turn around* is more common; *turn round* is British.

used to: *Used to* is the correct form, not *use to*; however, if the past tense is expressed with *did*, the form *use to* is required. **Examples:** *I used to go to the exercise room rather often. Didn't you use to go there often, too?*

way: The correct form is *way*, not *ways*. **Example:** *Graduation is still a long way off.*

The following pairs and groups of words are also sometimes confusing. Check a dictionary when there is any doubt about the meanings of these or other words.

accent, ascent, assent

adapt, adopt

advice, advise

aisle, isle

alley, ally

allowed, aloud

all together, altogether

allusion, illusion

altar, alter

anecdote, antidote

angel, angle

assistance, assistants

bare, bear

berry, bury

bibliography, biography

board, bored

brake, break

breath, breathe

buy, by

capital, capitol

cease, seize

cent, scent, sent

choose, chose

close, clothes

clothes, cloths

coarse, course

coma, comma

command, commend

confidant, confident

continual, continuous

cooperation, corporation

costume, custom

council, counsel

dairy, diary

dear, deer

deceased, diseased

decent, descent, dissent

device, devise

die, dye

dominant, dominate

elicit, illicit

emigrate, immigrate

eminent, imminent

empire, umpire

ensure, insure

envelop, envelope

fair, fare

feat, feet

finally, finely

flew, flu

flour, flower

formally, formerly

forth, fourth

gorilla, guerrilla

hardy, hearty

heal, heel

heard, herd

hole, whole

human, humane

incredible, incredulous

its, it's

know, no

later, latter

lead, led

lightening, lightning

loan, lone

magnate, magnet

mail, male

main, mane

meat, meet

miner, minor

moral, morale

of, off

pain, pane

pair, pear
pale, pail
passed, past
patience, patients
peace, piece
persecute, prosecute
personal, personnel
picture, pitcher
plain, plane
pray, prey
preposition, proposition
presence, presents
principal, principle
quiet, quite
rain, reign, rein
raise, raze
residence, residents
respectfully, respectively
right, rite, write
road, rode
role, roll

sail, sale
scene, seen
sense, since
soar, sore
stair, stare
steal, steel
suite, sweet
tail, tale
than, then
their, there, they're
thorough, threw, through
to, too, two
waist, waste
wait, weight
way, weigh
weak, week
weather, whether
which, witch
whose, who's
your, you're

Answers to Exercises

1. • My new English class begins at eight o'clock.
   • It lasts one hour.
   • There are students from seven countries in the class.
   • Our teacher has two rules.
   • Don't be late for class.
   • Please leave the classroom quietly.

2. • Our teacher gives us homework every day. *Or:* Every day our teacher gives us homework.
   • I do my homework in the library.
   • We are reading *My Name Is Aram.*
   • I don't have time for TV.
   • I am having trouble with this lesson.
   • Please help me with this. *Or:* Help me with this, please.

3. • It's easy to find our high school.
   • Go down this street, and turn left at the city hall.
   • Then drive across the river on Riverside Bridge.
   • The school is on the northwest corner of Winter Street and Freeway 94.
   • You'll see the new Northfield Municipal Stadium opposite the school.
   • You can park under the large oak tree on the north side of the school.

4. • has not
   • He has
   • can not, or cannot; it is
   • You had
   • He would
   • I will; I have

5. • ~~I like this city. I like this neighborhood.~~
   • The winters are mild. The summers are cool.
   • The shopping mall is not far from here, and it is easy to park there.
   • ~~The subway system here is very convenient, the fare is not very expensive.~~
   • My children can walk to school, or they can take the bus.
   • ~~The public pool is not far. Nor is it ever crowded.~~

6. • The city services are good, but (*or:* and, so) the taxes are high here.
   • The municipal zoo is free, and it is near our home.
   • There is little crime in this city, and (*or:* so) we are not afraid to go out alone at night.
   • People here drive slowly and carefully.
   • City employees can work from seven to three, or they can work from nine to five.
   • City employees have many days of vacation, yet (*or:* but, and) their salaries are very good.

7. • a kitchen table • a bicycle wheel • a fruit basket • a newspaper subscription • a basketball coach • a videotape

8. • Mr. Kim's new book • the dogs' owner (*or:* the dog's owner) • the Smiths' property • a motorcycle helmet • the bottom shelves • a library card • my books • a road map • France's history • the buses' (*or:* busses') drivers • a sports magazine • Bess's things

9. • I'm jogging now on Mondays, Wednesdays, and Fridays.
   • Playing tennis, skiing, and bowling are three healthful activities.

- I don't smoke or drink coffee anymore.
- I get a lot of exercise, and I go to bed early.
- I eat a lot of vegetables, but I don't like celery, broccoli, or onions.

10. • That new student is from Sri Lanka.
- He is?
- Yes, he is.
- Can he speak English?
- What do you think?
- When are you going to introduce me to him?

11. • Basically, there is no problem with your work, but you are late for class too often.
- I wonder if you could take notes for me in class on Monday. As you know, I can't come to school next week.
- Tuesday's test was difficult. In fact, I think I failed it.
- I can't afford to buy the textbook for class. Anyway, the teacher said it is not required.
- I'd like to skip chemistry lab today. Actually, I'd like to skip math class too.
- Mr. Brown is unpopular with the students, yet he is an internationally famous teacher.

12. • My birthday is on January 23, and my wife's birthday is on January 22.
- Anna-Marie was born on the 16th of December, but we had a party for her on the 20th.
- My best friend was born on a Saturday in February in 1956.
- Three people in my English class were born on the 23rd of this month, but one was born in 1976, and the other two were born in 1975.

- I'm having a birthday party on the 19th, and I'm sending you an invitation.
- I thought he was born on January 16, 1920, but he was born on January 16, 1919.

13. • Address
Mr. M. T. Feller, CEO
E. A. Crane Co.
203 N. Fourth St.
St. Paul, Minn. 55108 U.S.A.

- Itinerary
Dept. time: Mon., Jan. 31, 3:35 P.M.; Tokyo, Jpn.
Arr. time (approx.): Tues., Feb. 1, 6:40 A.M.; Helsinki, Fin.

- Ingredients
butter 200 g   flour 500 ml
sugar 350 g

- Class Schedule
first hr.: chem.; second hr.: econ.
third hr.: Ger.; fourth hr.: anthrop.

14. • Slow down! We're too close to that car. *Or:* Slow down! We're too close to that car!
- Please don't drive so fast.
Or: Please don't drive so fast!
- Watch out! Don't ever try that again.
Or: Watch out! Don't ever try that again!
- We can't park here. This is a bus stop. *Or:* We can't park here! This is a bus stop!
- You can let me off at the next corner. *Or:* You can let me off at the next corner!

15. • *How to Prepare for Exams*
- *A Guide to the Metropolitan Museum*
- *Be My Love*
- *Don't Look Behind You*
- *A Study of the Present Tense*
- *Just Between You and Me*

16. • At eleven o'clock, buses stopped running in this part of town. *Or:* Buses stopped running at eleven o'clock in this part of town. *Or:* Buses stopped running in this part of town at eleven o'clock.
    • Last year there was a transportation strike here too.
    • In today's newspaper there's an article about the strike.
    • At the top of the page, one of the bus drivers is interviewed. *Or:* One of the bus drivers is interviewed at the top of the page.
    • At the taxi company, drivers are working overtime. *Or:* Drivers are working overtime at the taxi company.
    • By tomorrow the bus strike will probably be over.

17. • I asked our guide about our itinerary.
    • Did he say anything about where we were going to have lunch?
    • You're going to the museum with us, aren't you?
    • The guide lent me his book *How to Enjoy Europe on a Small Budget.*
    • I also recommend *Are You Ready to Go Abroad?*
    • Have you read *How to Study a Foreign Language?*

18. • Yesterday's picnic wasn't much fun.
    • The temperature was in the 30s, and it was a very wet and windy day.
    • We weren't able to start a fire to cook anything.
    • We had some salad, but we couldn't barbecue the chicken.
    • We couldn't drink any juice because we didn't have any cups.
    • We sat in T. J.'s car and played some games and listened to our new CDs.

19. • There are several reasons why I have decided to move out of the college dormitory and look for an apartment. First of all, my room is very small. I don't even have room for my new computer desk. Secondly, the dormitory is very noisy in the evening, and I find it difficult to study there. Lastly, the college recently increased the dormitory fee. I am sure I can find a quiet and inexpensive apartment not too far from the campus.
    • Today was a very busy day for me. First, my friends gathered at my dormitory room at around 8 A.M. Then we packed all of my things into several boxes. Next, we put the boxes into my friends' cars, and after that, we drove to my new apartment. Then we unloaded the cars, unpacked the boxes, and put away all of my things. Finally, I made some pizza for my friends, and we sat around and watched television for a while.

20. • If you leave now, you'll be on time.
    • As soon as you get to the airport, give me a call.
    • Get something for Ken at the souvenir shop if you have time.
    • Even if you don't have time, you'd better get something for Ken.
    • I can't take you to the airport because I am busy this afternoon.
    • Although I can't take you to the airport, I can pick you up when you come back.

21. • Math is easy for my friends; it's difficult for me.
    • I like our math teacher; I don't care for the class.
    • History is my best subject; economics is my worst.

- I'm studying Chinese; I want to become an expert on the Far East.
- Foreign languages are easy for me; I think I'll work for the UN.
- Speaking Chinese is fairly easy; reading it is difficult.

22.
- My friend thought the movie was terrific; I thought it was boring.
- I really don't care to see films with a lot of violence; I don't like musicals either.
- I like to go to movies; I never watch them on TV.
- I don't go to movies often; they are expensive, and I am on a tight budget.
- Nobody likes the theater near the campus; the seats are very uncomfortable.
- I don't know whether I'll go to a movie next weekend; maybe I'll stay home and study.

23.
- We have some cinnamon in the cupboard; it is very old, however.
- This recipe is my grandmother's; therefore, it should be very good.
- We don't have any tea; consequently, I can't offer you any.
- This coffee is very weak; moreover, it is almost cold.
- I've already had two pieces of pie; I'll have another small piece, nevertheless.
- I've eaten too much; I am, therefore, going to skip dinner.

24.
- Fish is low in fat, and it is high in protein.
- Fresh fish is difficult to get in this part of the country; I would eat more of it, otherwise.
- Have some fried carrots, or eat one raw as a snack.
- Actually, I like vegetables; I do not eat a lot of fruit, however.

- Celery is an excellent food, but too much of it is not good for you.
- I usually avoid greasy foods; nevertheless, I sometimes have french fries with a hamburger.

25.
- The conductor of the orchestra, Rochus Feller, is a good friend of Carla and Steve's parents.
- Rochus Feller's brother is Martin Feller, the famous cellist.
- The Toronto Symphony Orchestra violinist Anna-Marie Hatano is related to Martin Feller.
- Carla and Steve's father has written one piece of music, a violin concerto.
- The Juilliard School, one of the most famous music schools in the country, is where Steve and Carla's parents met.
- The Austrian composer Mozart is Carla's favorite.

26.
- Our new music hall, which was completed in May, is already famous overseas.
- The person who designed the hall is Steve and Carla's uncle.
- Their uncle, who is only 29 years old, is well known for his work.
- The building across from the music hall is the old public library.
- The library, a white marble building, is a popular tourist attraction.
- People who have attended concerts in the new hall say that it is very comfortable.

27.
- I'd like to have Indian or North African food for lunch.
- Two restaurants near the campus serve North African dishes: the Cairo House and the Marrakesh.
- Jorge, Peter, Anna, and I had dinner at the Marrakesh last week.

- The Marrakesh is closed three days each week: Sundays, Mondays, and Tuesdays.
- The Cairo House restaurant has very good food, but it's rather expensive.
- There are two things that the Cairo House is famous for: namely, coffee and Egyptian bread.

28. • You came by car, didn't you? No, I came by bus.
- You'll be getting a ride, won't you? Yes, I think so.
- Grace usually comes to school on her bicycle, doesn't she? Yes, usually.
- You don't need a ride tomorrow, do you? No, that's OK.
- You wanted to borrow my car tonight, isn't that right? Yes, is that OK?

29. • On Monday morning I went to the dentist; on Monday afternoon I went to the bank; and Monday evening I made three long-distance calls to Mexico.
- On Wednesday, one of my busiest days this month, I had four difficult classes; I practiced for two hours with the basketball team; and I tutored my roommate in math for one hour.
- On Thursday I arranged basketball games for our team on Friday, the fourth; on Monday, the seventh; and on Thursday, the tenth.
- On Friday my brother called me from São Paulo; my sister called me from Rome; and I got a birthday card from a friend in Kyoto.
- On Saturday I slept late; I prepared for the marathon; and I finished the work I started last month.

- On Sunday, the day I usually spend relaxing, I had calls from Tokyo, Japan; Paris, France; Lagos, Nigeria; and Vietnam.

30. • an unusually heavy suitcase
- a large, red and yellow leaf
- a sick baby elephant
- a long, difficult novel
- a very important business letter
- a soft, old, comfortable chair

31. • some beautiful, delicate flowers
- an exciting children's program
- a complicated computer software program
- a brand-new, expensive sports car
- many very interesting books and magazines
- few modern office buildings

32. • Because of the warm weather, the snow was not very good.
- We enjoyed our ski trip in spite of the poor quality of the snow.
- In spite of the fact that we were all beginners, no one got hurt.
- Except for Kay, everyone wants to go skiing again next weekend.
- Kay wants to go bowling instead of skiing.
- Without skiing regularly, no one can learn to do it well.

33. • I can't tell you what she said to me.
- Did she say she was sorry?
- She said, "Oh, sorry." *Or:* She said: "Oh, sorry." *Or:* She said "Oh, sorry."
- I thought she said, "Don't worry." *Or:* I thought she said: "Don't worry." *Or:* I thought she said "Don't worry."

- On the phone last night, she said, "My mother said to apologize."
  Or: On the phone last night, she said: "My mother said to apologize."
- What did you say to her?

34. • Have you read Martin's book *The Life of a Chameleon*?
   - Lars said he read it in one day.
   - If the book is at the library, Anna said she'd read it.
   - Martin said he would be happy to sign the book for us.
   - The chapter "Chameleons as Pets" is very interesting.
   - Did you say "Chameleons"?
     Or: Did you say: "Chameleons"?
     Or: Did you say, "Chameleons"?

35. • We're going to lose the game; (*or:* :) our best player is in the hospital.
   - Armando is a school hero: (*or:* ;) he scored ten points in the game.
   - You're really not interested in attending the football game tonight, are you?
   - That's what I don't like about baseball: (*or:* ;) the games last so long.
   - Listen to what I heard today: our teacher has a black belt in karate.
   - I know why he doesn't play basketball; (*or:* :) he doesn't like the coach.

36. • av/e/nue • item • equal • awk/ward
   - im/pos/sible • text/book • sleep/ing
   - fit/ting • cared • ef/fort • opened
   - al/ways • ra/dio • self-/taught
   - teacher • com/puter • uni/ver/sity

37. • Ali's new eight-hundred-dollar bicycle was stolen from his house last night.
   - Someone entered a first-floor window of Ali's house while Ali was at the gym playing basketball.

- A neighbor said the burglar was about 180 centimeters tall and was wearing a white-and-yellow sweater.
- Another neighbor said she saw a 180-centimeter-tall, strange-looking man walking around in front of Ali's house a few days ago.
- Fortunately, Ali found his bicycle on the school grounds today.
- Unfortunately, the badly damaged bicycle will be impossible to repair.

38. • I know you don't care for horror movies—but I do.
   - Let's rent another video tomorrow—if you don't have anything better to do.
   - *The Third Man*—which is my favorite film—is showing at the Grand next week.
   - I highly recommend the Grand Theater—it's air-conditioned.
   - Ken enjoyed the movie for only one reason—the scenes of Vienna.
   - Marc goes to movies regularly—in fact, he sees a film at least twice a week.

39. • Lincoln High School . . . is the oldest school in the city.
   - Several graduates of the school have become famous. . . .
   - At a recent graduation ceremony, the mayor spoke to the students . . . about changes in high school education in the United States.
   - The mayor also said that . . . students had not changed . . . since he attended Lincoln High School.
   - The students enjoyed the mayor's speech. . . .
   - After the ceremony the mayor joined the new graduates at a banquet. . . .

40. • I sometimes find good recipes in the Sunday edition of the newspaper.
    • The pie Jean made was just good; the pie Lorraine made was <u>very</u> good.
    • I like Thai food, but I don't care for <u>dom yam</u>.
    • Some of my favorite recipes are from the cookbook <u>Recipes From Around the World</u>.
    • There is a good recipe for pizza in the chapter on Italian food.
    • I'm still not used to using the metric system in recipes.

41. • Two of the city's three lakes are near my apartment.
    • My neighborhood is only 12 miles from the airport, or about 45 minutes by car.
    • The population of the city, which is 289,651, has decreased by .3 percent over the past 24 months.
    • Recently more than $18 billion has been spent on a new subway system here.
    • The basic fare for the subway is two dollars.
    • A ceremony to inaugurate the new subway will be held at 9:00 A.M. on June 3.

Index

5935